FAST & EASY TO LEARN !

LIE DETECTION Vs MENTALISM

You will be focusing on some very effective and dangerous techniques and you will be able to detect them if they are exercised against you.

PHILIPPE KAIZEN

LIE DETECTION

vs

MENTALISM

**Pragmatic strategies for detecting lies
and enhancing your skills.**

Philippe Kaizen

CONTENTS

How shall this book benefit you.

If you have bought my first book, then you have already gained some good competencies. But through this, you are about to impregnate yourself with a **highly-advanced** section on all types of manipulations. This is otherwise known as, "Mentalism". Thus, you will be focusing on some very effective and dangerous techniques. Taking into consideration these invaluable with attention, you will naturally be able to detect them in case they are exercised against you.
But yet again, you must first broaden your potential in determining the body language of another in order to discern him better and much faster.
In a nutshell, this is the theme of my blog, and eventually, you shall attain a notch above, against lies, liars and fraudsters of all types.

I wish you a nice reading.

Philippe Kaizen.

Chapter 1

INTRODUCTION

But what is the role of Mentalism in a book about lie detection? Why mentalism?

What is mentalism? You must certainly be pondering upon one of these questions. If you search its definition on the Internet, you might perhaps end up with the wrong idea.

Very often, this is invoked by my blog readers or during friendly conversations, the same questions always seems to come up: " but, do you know anything about mentalism? Do you do what Patrick Jane (from the TV series, The Mentalist) does, when he detects lies? " And so on. I wasn't aware of this drama and wasn't in my interest to watch it either. But at the end of the fiftieth time I decided to deal with this mentalism once and for all.
After several months of research and scrutiny on the question, below is my definition.

Mentalism is the art of manipulating people. To manipulate another using various psychological tricks as was the suggestion, the misappropriation of attention which is also and principally, the art to feign psychic powers. What are these powers?
Powers such as " mind reading " or reading another's thoughts for example, but it also involves foresight or the art of predicting the future.

Two weeks after drafting the article " Predict reactions through lie detection " on my blog in October, I was contacted by a friend whom I had not seen for quite a long time. This man, Pierre, is a psychic. It wasn't his job but he gives "consultations" only among his close friends. He can only be consulted through a recommendation from one of his friends and he is renowned to be very good indeed.

So, he contacts me: " *Philippe, I just read your article and was allured by one thing on which you spoke in particular, and that was, 'cold reading of a situation'. You render some short-time frozen snapshots of people in your article, even if your theory is only concerned with gestures. Were you aware that, this is exactly what is called, cold reading? That is a tool used by many psychics. This is a topic worth elaborating on."*

After several weeks of e-mail exchanges and researches from my side, Pierre decided to show me some manipulation techniques related to cold reading. I was then introduced to a women, a friend of his, (without informing her of our experiment's objective) who was also a psychic, and was capable of depicting present or future happenings. Next, he put forward a challenge to divulge if she was saying the truth or not by arranging a session with her. The results are stated farther in this book... I guarantee you, that having read my book, you will be competent in taking a set of cards, or tarot for example, and predict someone's future successfully !

I am not about to enlighten you on reading the future through tarots, which is actually far from my mind. But once you master all these manipulation techniques which we shall practice together throughout this book, you shall notice that it is entirely possible to do so, as well. These techniques can be further exercised in various situations of our life.
They can empower you to foresee certain events and thus, take (productive) decisions. They shall tempt you to apply yourself in very interesting subjects such as human relations, communication but especially in understanding another (and of course, yourself as well). They will serve you as a very effective training ground in determining the body language and will also allow you to improve your skills in lie detection, which is obviously, the purpose of this book.

Needless to say, you shall also assimilate in detecting these manipulations so that they will have no effect on you. These are therefore the reasons as to why I titled this book:

"Lie Detection versus Mentalism"

To make things clear, I do rely on the fact that there are clairvoyances or psychic powers. In my opinion on the question, I perceive that it exists and that people are capable of "determining" "something" in which we all seem connected... Have you come across anyone who has had intuitions or presentiments about something, who had thought of exactly the same thing as you at the same time and then laughed once you noticed it? At some moment in life, why did you decide to remain at your own precise decision when all other aspects lead you to do the opposite? Why did you follow your possibilities when you could have done better in following your intuitions? When you were determined to achieve an aspiration, and you strongly urged for something, have you not noticed that somehow, events seemed to turn out to be lucky? For example, a completely unexpected meeting or an impressive idea that suddenly springs up and contributes in finding a solution to your problem.

Your intuition contributes in fulfilling your ultimate goal that you have set for yourself, successfully without failure. But have you ever wondered why? Dear reader, Do you aspire in having, a latent psychic capacity that allows you "to feel" things? Or had I already begun to manipulate you?

As I said before, I do rely on the fact that there are clairvoyances or psychic powers, I think that they exist but I must warn you that 95 % of the people appearing as clairvoyants, psychics, etc., are fraudsters. And we shall soon see how.

I reassure you that this book does not solely deal with this theme. As mentioned above, understanding these techniques shall acquire in you a preferable proficiency in determining another's body language and also in detecting lies, in a better way. These techniques are also used by swindlers, commercials, or sellers of all kinds who will effortlessly try to sell you something at the highest price.

Here is a summary of the various chapters that we are about to embark on together.

Chapter two, A fundamental recollection, which will update you on lie detection techniques. In order to master these techniques constructively and in detail I would like to advise you however, to read my first book.

Otherwise, you may still acquire it through this chapter, it is always helpful in being ready for the worse.

Chapter three, will embark you on the profoundness of my article that I wrote in October 2010 on my blog. It will mainly focus on, the recent developments of a radical reading technique of another.
Extremely compelling, I have been using this technique for a long time in order to avoid being surprised, but moreover, it helps me in the anticipation of certain events. This cold reading will serve as a transitional introduction, towards the fascinating realm of cold reading found in the next chapter.

Chapter four, shall introduce you to the tremendous realm of cold reading . If you long to become a psychic, this is the chapter you were waiting for... Principally, if you discern that the cold reading technique in the previous chapter is quite similar to this section as well, then bear in mind that here, you shall emerge into an art form to which there is very little research sources. The chief origin of this art is the world of clairvoyance. Thus, I am going to give you, the utmost of my experience on this subject, through the investigations I have carried out with my friend, Pierre. There is sure to be lots of action...

After fully reading this chapter, you will naturally be aware of the manipulation attempts of this kind that can most probably be directed towards you.

In **chapter five** we shall approach several mental manipulation techniques.

Firstly, the technique of "influence of appearances" in which you will deal with the detection that you had done earlier. Appearances are very often made up.

Next, we shall scrutinize on the concepts of thought manipulation and attention manipulation.

Do you know anything on the planning technique? And the one that leads to forgetfulness, of the person who speaks to you, of his own words?

I expect that this information satisfies you and therefore, without further delay ,I invite you to embark forward...

Chapter 2

LIE DETECTION FUNDAMENTALS

If I was to summarize my lie detection theory, I would declare that it articulates around the following three points:

1) Limbic Reactions and Emotions

2) Gestures and Reactions associated with the 1st point

3) Reactions related to Logic and Common Sense

If you have already read my book on lie detection, you can skip onto the next chapter, otherwise, do not hesitate to continue reading this chapter synthesis. However I shall describe briefly on some techniques that can be used in a recruitment processes, as long as want to read.

Bear in mind that all the techniques of lie detection are not brought out through this book, only those concerned with manipulation techniques.
Limbic reactions are derived from your brain. They come from a part of the brain that controls feelings and memory. This part possesses a sort of survival system that controls our reactions during an unexpected incident.

For example, if you see a car about to bump into you while crossing the street, you will have what is known as, a" reflex " in order to dive or escape from the vehicle as fast as you can. If you accidentally place your hand on the heating plate that you forgot to switch off, after having cooked this delicious plate of steak, you would not let it rest there for a fraction of a second any longer. Another example, imagine that you have climbed onto the rooftop of a fifty-storeyed building, and you move closer towards the edge, opening out into space. Suddenly, someone close by, pushes you very slightly and you are almost about to fall down. Do you think you wouldn't react? In fact, it is not your body that reacts but your limbic brain which immediately transmits signals or orders to your body and forces it to react.
The limbic brain is the peak of feelings. Once you feel a strong

emotion, this part of the brain will force a reaction, known as a reflex. It is almost impossible to control this. This is why gestures betray thoughts in lie detection. Thoughts are therefore, closely related with, feelings felt at a particular moment. If you directly ask from your interlocutor about something that would distract him, you will succeed in surprising him. Surprised means emotion.

And emotion means a limbic reaction and thus a gesture.

If this gesture, of your interlocutor, is immediate, like a reflex due to a surprise, then, you can conjecture that it was the result of his limbic brain. Thus, you are witnessing a true reaction and not a simulated reaction.

You can easily diffuse the difference between these two, for example when you offer someone a present . If he smiles almost simultaneously, you can conclude that it was a sincere reaction. If, on the other hand the same person takes a little time to smile, thus you can easily determine it to be a simulation. All these techniques are based upon feelings. The person smiling having received your present felt a deep emotion and his limbic brain transforms this into a physical reaction. If the person does not appreciate your present at all, what do you think he will he do next?

Yes, having "processed" the shock, he will next try to persuade you that the present cheers him up by feigning a feeling of enjoyment. This is the clear discrepancy between a sincere limbic reaction and a feigned reaction. Meanwhile, something else is also going on before this false reaction. In order to discern what this is, let us return to the mechanism of feelings.

Emotion means a brain limbic reaction and thus a gesture. Through this gesture, I am also implicating on the face, not just the arms, legs or any other part of the body. We shall certainly intricate on this a little farther.

The person who did not like your present, will feel a dissatisfactory feeling (since she does not like it very much). As a matter of fact, imagine that you decided to offer your girlfriend a watch for she has never been punctual (your girlfriend, not the watch). You've already mentioned about it to her more than once. Early in the morning you present the watch in a small square box (which strangely looks exactly like those small ring boxes). You expect her face to be brightened, as it's been a long time since she hoped that you will keep your promise. But once opened, great is the disappointment. And great becomes the emotion. Who said emotion means... You know the rest. If your girlfriend, in trying to hide her disappointment, tries to feign a happiness in receiving the present, there will be a limbic reaction which will be demonstrated through her facial expression, a spatial gesture or a closed expression.

I always joke on regular unpunctual girlfriends. What I really want to express with the help of this example, is that whatever maybe the emotion, whether positive or negative, it will certainly generate a reaction from the body.
And, if this reaction is immediate, hence, you can resolve it to be sincere at the moment.
Let see now these famous physical reactions. They are categorized into three parts:

1) Spatial Type Reactions

2) Notions of Openness and Closeness

3) Notions of Self-Massage

Spatial Type Reactions

These reactions can be separated in to two different groups. The first group includes movements in space following an event generating a reaction. The second group includes postures that we further settle on to surprise. These postures can be present before an event, progress during, and modify again later. For an example when you have an appointment for a job interview. You can settle yourself in a certain posture, before meeting the HR manager, depending on your stress level at the time. Your posture can then progress during the interview based on the questions put forward and if you are comfortable or not, in answering them at the moment. You can then adopt another posture once the interview ends.

We shall elaborate more on stress when we deal with post--limbic reactions (physical or oral).

You will ultimately discern that it is unnecessary to assimilate dozens or even hundreds of positions or postures just to detect lies.

But why use, "spatial" ?

Because these reactions are directly connected with space that you occupy in a given situation. Let us take two examples.

You are in a restaurant, seated, and furthermore in charming company. Or standing, leaned at a pub counter, it actually doesn't matter. However, you feel good with this person's presence. You feel an emotion bound to this state of pleasure. From the viewpoint of using the space, you might tend to get closer to this person. And to do so, you will move your chair closer , bend forward, in brief, you will occupy more space in the person's direction. Would you adopt this same spatial position if the person in front of you was your boss? And if this person brought you some bad news? And while you least expect it, the person seated opposite or next to you remarks: " I am aware *that you have lied to me recently* ". If you had really lied to this person and if the statement surprises you, the emotion felt at this very moment is going to move your gestures, you might want to escape from this potential danger.

Thus, you shall retreat. If you were leaned against this person you will bounce back. You will certainly say something like" What? " then comes the time to process your surprise. And a stressful condition is going to settle on your head and, to keep well away from this threat, you will sit at the very end of your chair. You will also release other signals using your face, arms or legs, which we shall elaborate on, a little farther.

That was a perfect example that unfolds the posture progress's with time. At the beginning, you feel a positive impression , and you are even leaned towards this person. Next, a surprise! A bristly question, followed by a declining reaction. And as the third step, you are under pressure as you are now entangled in a problem and need to handle it wisely.

Thus, stress contributes in retreating from the spatial position in order to keep you unconsciously away from this threat.

These three positions in space can therefore be represented in the following way: release, freeze and finally, aggression. In the case of the restaurant and your charming company, you must have understood that the fact of leaning forward does not correspond to an aggression. Thus, a brief adjustment must be inflicted since it is the reaction that unfortunately occurs in the couple's story. For example, the partner may be orally violent or aggressive. This type of person would not necessarily be retreating to escaping from the danger but rather try and knock down the pressure in an aggressive way. Example: " What!? How dare you say? That I lied to you?! How dare you call me a liar?! ". This is a kind of misappropriation in the subject where the aggressor is effortlessly trying to make the other feel guilty. And I will not elaborate on how emotionally charged the atmosphere is during this kind of behaviour which generally shock the other person having dared to challenge his authority.

Notions of Openness and Closeness.
I shall take a real-life example which you doubtlessly would have already experimented : public transport.

It is the peak hour there are lots of people. I know this is unbelievable and not realistic, but let us imagine that you somehow found a seat. There are a lot of people. How are you going to sit down? How are the other people going to sit down? Do you make a cross? That is to have arms wide apart from every side on the seat, legs pushed forward and wide apart ? **This is a**

(completely) opened position. You expose yourself to other people. In fact, it's seems as if you assure mental access to the sensitive parts of your body to other people around. Do you really do this in public transport?

No, I doubt it, I don't do so myself. Something urges us to protect ourselves, to protect the sensitive parts of our body. We have no intention in being in danger. This is why, practically, everyone in public transport have, legs and/or arms crossed, for example. But it can also be a slight orientation of the body on the other hand, which depicts, the dislike in facing another directly. And it can also be a handbag, a book or quite a different object sensibly placed on your knees as you sit. The book can be between your crossed arms and your body as if you have it tightened in your arms. You can stand, leaning on one of the train doors and have joint hands or arms, fallen forward in order to secure your privacy.

These examples symbolizes perfectly, the notion of a **closed position**.

I would like to draw your attention towards a very interesting position as I have used this with the closed position for a long time. Always imagine the public transport situation, a person is leaned against the door, hand in pockets and a leg crossing the other. Is this a closed position? Well not by definition. It would rather be the opposite. Practically, crossing a leg while standing, means to have your total balance only on one leg. In public transport, wagons always tend to move in all directions, therefore, it's rare not to lose balance. If a person balances on a single leg, and is not afraid of falling, this position thus exhibits a notion of assurance rather than the will to close. I rather agree. The same position, but this time would represent a closure, where the person is leaned against the door, but from the side, (he is leaned on his shoulder) and would remain well-balanced. This is in fact what keeps this person away from being in danger since he is aware that there is no reason to be afraid of losing balance. The crossed leg therefore indicates a position of closure in this particular case. When we are in a room having no interest in being there, our sole determination is to : leave this room as fast as possible, here, we sometimes, adjust to a certain posture. This is an incident that might have occurred to you more than once, during those boring working meetings. We always find ourselves directing towards the exit. Simply.

This concludes the notion of openness and closeness of our body. We are now going to bring them all together with the third notion.

Notions of Self-Massage

This act of self-massage is the massaging process done during a stressful situation. This is the reaction that I qualify as post or pre-limbic. Which means that it takes place before or after the first reflex reaction that we express once we are surprised. But, the cause remains the same, **feelings**.

For example, you are going for a job interview.

Seated in the terrace of a coffee shop a few minutes before proceeding towards the door threshold. It can also be during the interview, after a difficult question, and you are under a certain amount of stress. When you are stressed, anxious, or worried about something in particular, you go round in circles, and wait for that fateful moment when you must actually deal with this situation. The feelings felt at this moment will effect on how you react. Besides, the postures of openness and closeness about which we just spoke, you will strongly feel the longing to release this tension, and try to be calm for a second. So, what do we do when we want to release the tension out of something? We massage it.

Have you never caught yourself rubbing legs as you sit? As if you are practicing a massage technique to relax?

Have you never held your forearms to rub back and forth with your thumb to relax yourself? This is the self-massage reaction.

Thus, we have explored on the three main points of reactions in our body: movements of spatial orders, notions of openness and closeness and notions of self-massage. These three characteristics can be brought together into one situation. Let us take the job interview example once more and make use of it to scrutinize on some techniques used in the recruitment procedures. The company secretary welcomes you and takes you into a room where the interview is to be conducted. You take a seat and wait until several people who are also ready for this interview have finished theirs.

This is a very important job for you and you are intended to acquire it for yourself.

This job is not yet reserved, since other candidates are also yet to be interviewed. Even if you are self-confident, unless being completely insensible of the pressure, you will still feel a small stress or pressure. Thus, this will result from a reaction from your body. You may sit down crossing your legs or arms and by doing that you will rendering a slight impression of closure to the recruiter who shall unexpectedly enter into the room.

Some recruiters, especially conscientious companies, are insiders of postures and will observe you during the course of the interview. You might have often heard about first impressions, thus if you reciprocate with an image of a very closed person, this impression can linger around during the whole interview. Let me give you a small trick (that I used to do myself during my interview), the secretary who welcomes leaves you waiting in a room where there are glass walls (transparent in fact). The recruiter might pass near this room several times and observe your posture. You had not seen him before, and thus, you are unaware that it is "him" (the recruiter) who is passing repeatedly looking discreetly at this room. Another recruitment technique is to keep you waiting.

Very often I had noticed the HR manager, the project manager and the psychologist never arrived on time. Always between twenty to thirty minutes of delay. This is very often intentionally done to increase the candidate's pressure, and maybe even to try and lose his patience. And if you become tired of waiting, I can guarantee you that it is instantly revealed from your facial expressions and your general behavior. Not very suitable for a job dealing with stress management.

What will you do then? Try to adjust your reactions? You might have heard this strategy earlier but, in fact it doesn't contribute much. As a matter of fact, let's continue this interview further. The recruiter arrives, you are seated in front of him, and he is reading your curriculum vitae. At once, you remember a tip you found on the Internet telling you to adjust yourself by forcing an open posture, not to cross arms or legs or to sit up straight, etc...

Two things, the first one, this happens when you tend to concentrate on your false posture so much, which is actually not the true feeling you feel, then you will try to give the recruiter a freezed impression. Even in doing so, you pointlessly try to control yourself when you really aren't yourself. The second, this is when the recruiter will start questioning you, you will concentrate more on his questions that you completely forget your posture.

Leaving a candidate in a room can have the following additional effect.

The fact of being in a room alone can give the impression that nobody is watching and thus, it is unnecessary to force an image any longer. So, our normal stressful position are replaced and a more or less closed posture is adopted. It is thus, at this moment that I enter... where I can have an a « raw » picture of the candidate's state of mind before the interview.

We shall analyze more in detail in the next chapter together with my cold reading technique.

The interview continues, and the recruiter decides to surprise you slightly with some questions like: " In your opinion, how can you constructively benefit us, compared to the other candidates that we have already received? "or else" what influenced you to leave your former employment? Were you dissatisfied? Did you have trouble with your hierarchy? ". Hence, the list of questions continues (yet, not very disagreeable) which will provoke your reactions. Your limbic brain will be ready to go into action and it is, at this moment that you must adjust your space with the recruiter (spatial reactions). With regard to the forward position, you might even even seek refuge under your chair. You might hold your pen in your hands so as to create a barrier between both of you and guard yourself from his questions. You may move your arms closer (whereas, before they were clearly settled on both sides of the table). You may even cross them, in short, you close   yourself.

As you ponder on the answer to this stressful question, you begin to, for an instance, tighten your grip on the pen, and roll it between your thumb and the forefinger (this will consequently massage your fingers and relax you). You may also, place a hand on your forearm and rather massage with your thumb. Briefly, you strongly risk in self-massaging.

Thus, you have just read an example demonstrating the three reaction types in a single interview.

From the viewpoint of the recruiter or the lady who has just remarked her husband with " I am aware that you have deceived me ", these physical reactions have a particular significance: they seem to related to the question asked, possibly, have you done something that deserves a blaming, which would, by chance make you afraid? Are you hiding anything? Is there anything that you are supposed to speak to me about and you haven't?

Now, we will rush through the third reaction type. These reactions does not actually fall under the category of "nonverbal" but in the contrary, these are grouped as "verbal". These signals are explored in detail in my previous book , and thus, we shall not procrastinate on this further. If I were to summarize these reactions, I would declare that they are all categorized under "common sense and logic".

Techniques that are amply used in lie detection and especially those that must be paid direct attention are, **the change of subject, answering in various levels, generalization and taking**

time. In fact, 'change of subject' is one of the leading techniques used by liars. A lying person becomes surprised by a question that might distract him, which can put him under pressure. He will then effortlessly try to release this pressure and speak in the best possible verbal method to..... change the subject. There are several straightforward methods to change the subject. Doubtlessly, you must have noticed already, sudden changes in subjects, normally followed by an awkward or improper question, during your conversations. Two even more subtle methods are: using an unexpected event that has nothing to do with your conversation (oh, I just saw an U.S Army boat parked in the street). Or continue with an element that was present in the annoying question and concentrate on the foregoing discussion thread. In order to aptly comprehend this idea, 'change of subject', put yourself in the shoes of a lying person. You have just told a big lie to someone around you. Suddenly, when you least expected it, this person proceeds towards and returns to the same conversation that angers you.

You are once again under pressure. How can you draw yourself out of this? How can you actually prevent the other person from discovering the truth? You might try everything under your power to steer away from this danger, in fact, you will try to change the subject as carefully as possible if attainable.

The technique , 'answering in various levels' is not literally a technique but precisely, a logical mechanism. The core of the mechanism of these answers, that a lying person can reply to you with, are further in his details.

Obviously, in everyday life, it is advisable to be concerned about your interlocutor's personality. If he is preferably a laconic person in his words, then, there won't be much detail in his answers. Thus, you will necessarily have to deal with this person directly and ask him for explanations on the annoying subject. Laconic or not, the person will be obliged to render some explanation to defend his side of the story. If on the other hand, your interlocutor is of an eccentric nature, where he is used to speak for hours on what he does during evenings, and in the contrary, he provides his answers with hardly any detail, then that must draw your attention. The opposite can be also true.

Life is full of habits and routines, and any abrupt change in these patterns, must be noticed. Need not necessarily be suspicions of course, but at least noticed. Once these parameters are ready, you will be competent in analyzing the various level of details in your interlocutor's answers.

You may convince yourself that as much as the answers are detailed, they bear truthfulness. With this thought in mind, I strongly object to the following answers : yes and no.

Let us take for an example, an evening spent with your interlocutor, or with his friends. If this evening was spent well, then there will be details, for sure. Indeed, if you have gone through something, you become capable of elaborating on it. It is logic.

And also, on the contrary, if you did not spend the evening with your friends, then you won't be able to give details. Especially, if you are surprised by the question. This is actually the subject of my lie detection method, surprising the other in order to draw out a reaction. Indeed, if you surprise your interlocutor, this will generate some stress in him for he now has to immediately fabricate an answer to your annoying question. And what exactly is done at times like these?

It is answered with short sentence, perhaps by even picking up certain words from the question itself. Either to gain more time, or to render more reliability to the answer. But particularly, he will not get into detail since mistakes can occur, possibly by being too inconsistent, and forgetting what is already spoken of.

What's to be done when your interlocutor have prepared his answer?

It is up to you to acquire a detailed version of the facts.

On the other hand, our purpose will be to detect any possible lie in a discreet, furtive way, without your interlocutor realizing it.

In order to to do so, you must hunt through this detailed answer for feelings, feelings felt by your interlocutor during the evening. Perhaps, you must have already had the notion of deciphering a hollow automated speech.

As if in fact, memorized. It is exactly, the lack of emotion in his speech that made you decipher this suspicion.

Therefore, now, you may have a good conception on the accuracy of an answer based on your interlocutor's feelings. But still, what if it contains feelings of the people present in this evening. What is your opinion on the following sentences, that are said in two different ways?

Sentence one: " I told him not to do that "
Sentence two: " I told him: " no, don't do that! " "

The second sentence is comparatively personal, as if the person holds responsibility for his own words. If you were the lying person and you had never told the other these words you might ideally be inclined to build up a less personal sentence. Thus, this second utterance can intensify the sincerity of the answer.

There is an additional attribute that you may conjecture in the above sentences. That is that it is very rare to find negative events spoken. The reasons for this are quite simple , you may risk yourself in making a mistake by not recalling what was negative in your flawed story. But what you also risk is that your interlocutor might want to know more about this and thus ask you more questions regarding this matter. What, you should comprehend here is that, you are forced to fabricate some real time new story right in front of him. Thus, you venture in cheating yourself through gestures or answer abruptly, in a very laconic way.

"Generalization" which includes an answer disclosing oneself impersonally, but this is also an effective way of changing the subject. A short example of a sentence articulated by a lady to her husband: *" you weren't with your friends the other evening, admit it! I know that you are lying to me!."*

What!? How dare you accuse me like that!? Aren't you ashamed? You are well aware that I am usually   not like that! I am a man with some integrity!".

In this retort, we also find the final relief used by liars: the attempt to take more time.

As we inquire into this sentence, we find three techniques: the first one, 'taking time'. It enables to think quickly on a solution to escape from this burden. This leads to questions for answers to questions again. Next, we find, 'generalization', " *You are well aware that I am usually not like that* etc. ". The third technique is an attempt to make the other guilty, which will lead to a certain aggressiveness. The purpose is to discourage the other by force (of words) in order to exploit for another round of arguing. Finishing the conversation is also a way to change the subject and then, start speaking about something quite different. This technique rendering multiple causes takes place not only when dealing with couples but throughout, on the TV, for example during discussions based on politics, when the guest in question finds himself perplexed by a sensitive question. Finally, in order to conclude this chapter expounding on some fundamental recollections on certain lie detection techniques, I will give you a small summary of what we spoke.

Our body responds to feelings that are controlled through our brain. It makes gestures directly bound to these feelings. Our face reacts, as our arms, legs, and the whole body moves.

It moves through space, gets closer to the source of the emotion, or steers away from it. It opens and closes depending on the prevalent threat ahead of us. Our body positions itself according to our disposition. We can be stressed before, during or after a particular event.

We will now proceed forward, to the next factual chapter guiding towards my method, of cold reading another...

Chapter 3

COLD READING

Here are some privileges that my cold reading technique can promote to your well-being: you become competent in recognizing someone through his disposition within seconds.

You will be proficient in anticipating the possible reactions of you or your interlocutor and acquire the best decisions depending on the situation.
You will noticeably enhance your ascertainment in the body language of others as this exercise requires a certain training and thus, you will be forced to think very fast.

An effective cold reading will also lead you to avoid being surprised in many situations. During my article "anticipate on reactions through lie detection", I presented a case of a strike in a large French company which could result in a series of dismissals. The aggressive approach of the company's investors and the CEO had been suspended due to the fast discernment of their dispositions. Likewise, we will scrutinize together on several real life situations where I have applied cold reading. I will also be reiterating a part of a critical situation that continued for several weeks in one of the branches of the company that I work for.
In addition I will use an interview analysis that I made about a person that is often in the American media while I'm writing these lines
Then, it would be easier for you to adjust it to yourself with all the situations that you'll be dealing with.

Voluntary communication. This is the concept that we will be incorporating to our cold reading technique in order to optimize it.

Voluntary communication is the deliberated will to convey a perception to another. It is ideally interpreted as 'the way we dress', in the same manner that we shall witness in the following example. Communication focuses in rendering an impression to the other with the intention of deceiving him via this supposition,

by reading the situation. This variable must be significantly considered in cold reading and confronted by determining the body language of our target. And eventually, you will notice how seriously often this technique is applied by politicians, specialists, etc...
In fact, for any media display but also during business conferences and even in the area of seduction.

Well, as a matter of fact, it happens as soon as there is an inclination to transmit an image.

Action !

To stay short, all the employees of a particular branch of a company, are waiting for the coming of two investors about future dismissals that was to take place a few months later.

They had not yet arrived. First thing to be done, get rid of the idea about how these investors are going to look like.

Do not ask yourself this question, remain impartial on this matter. Why? Simply because of the discrepancy that could build up between your perception and the reality which could influence you more than you believe. Everything is in the visual impact, your brain will capture and record the image that you'll see before you'll even know it.

You may start imagining these investors, all in black, suits (black), wearing dark glasses and a strange pen with a red light on top of their jacket pocket ! And unexpectedly, they might arrive in a pair of shorts and Hawaiian shirts! The impact on your brain will be much stronger as the difference between your idea and the reality becomes bigger. Therefore, be attentive.

The only issue is that **as your brain invariably captures whatever it sees**, and since you have seen these people in

Hawaiian shirts during the course of the interview right in front of you, this will contribute in strengthening a conveyance of an unconcerned impression. This is a subtle and perpetual influence to which you might not pay any attention, but your brain will, and it continues to record the information.

Therefore, desist from trying to guess what they will look like, conjecture only of one single thing, examine their postures / behavior as they enter the room and settle down. Then, observe their dresses or the way they are dressed.
An example on the foregoing social conflict.

The company's investors and the director enter the room and settle down. All the employees are at the bottom of the room facing the trio.

Tables are arranged so as to form a big oval filling the room. The trio is positioned on the opposite side. One investor on the side of the oval (not facing the employees), the other one sits opposite to him and thus has the employees in front of him and the director sits facing the first investor. Thus he is also not facing the employees.

Here is the complete example on the cold reading of the first investor. There are significant four factors to be concerned. Firstly, you had not attempted to guess what he would look like before he arrived. Secondly, derive an analysis on his visual impact. He is a man of about fifty years, probably about fifty five. He has gray hair, wears small glasses and continues to smile. Next, he has removed his jacket before entering and is thus wearing a white, slightly unbuttoned shirt. Through his sleeve, an old small watch with hand could be seen, discreet yet matches perfectly with the rest. This man conveys a relaxed, pleasant and friendly impression. **Your brain has recorded and validated this impression for quite a long time already.**

You might not notice but nevertheless you feel an impression of sympathy towards this man. Quite the contrary for why he is here. Thirdly, contemplate on the background of this gentleman. This investor represents an investment firm, and he is thus used to socialize with preferably, (big) customers, to discuss, negotiate, or even convince other investors. The gentleman's age thus implies a certain amount of professional experience on the job and communication. You may therefore perceive that this pleasant face and his general visual impact are the outcomes of a voluntary communication.

Fourthly, you must apply all your attention on his posture and his body language, which will greatly assist in gaining a better conception on his actual disposition. Bear in mind that disposition does not often travel in the same direction as visual communication!

However, even if this man is pleasant, he rejects to sit in front of his employees. Previously, we came across someone embarrassed, having something to hide, is not willing to face the threat, and if he is obliged, he would possibly switch his body to a side. That is a common way of protecting oneself. He is seated normally, neither too forward nor too retreated , yet, he is moving his pen in quite a nervous way.

Gestures seem to be sudden and continues lowering the hand, as though something is bothering him. Precisely, he continues to hold the pen between his hands during the course of the meeting so as to create a defense between him and the employees. If you put together the three facts: analysis of the impression that he wants to convey, the appropriate background of this person, and his posture, you will notice that there are certain contradictions. This person wants to convey an image that is contradicted through his gestures, thus, it can be concluded that he will probably be bringing forward some annoying affairs during this interview and can even reveal a personality in contrast with his relaxed appearance. This first cold reading should arouse your circumspection against this man.

Let us now examine the second investor's visual communication. He is much younger, just around thirty. He is dressed in a suit or tie (black) but also does not remove his jacket, which is completely buttoned. He doesn't smile and his face is tightened. The visual impact that our brain receives on this man, is of a closed man, who has no interest in joking and who will not necessarily be opened to discussion. What can we declare on his supposed background? This man is young, and perhaps has started working in this firm quite recently. Therefore, he might not have gained much experience from his associates and probably, he might carry out a communication error. Is he possibly, a young aspirational man endeavoring to be imperative, and impress the debate, while revealing his proficiency in the eyes of his peer? Two branches of reflection that, once taken into consideration, may, prevent you from being surprised. What about his body language?
He is seated in front of the employees. Is this a mistake or is he trying to dominate the employees by thrusting upon the center?
Both these branches of reflection stated above can be clearly discerned. He has piled up a bunch of documents in front of him and then crosses his arms over it. This is the "defense "gesture with the purpose of building up a protection zone(similar to eradicating himself from everything he has no intention of listening to). All of his glances will be directed towards his documents. Hence, he shall hardly need to glance at his employees.
His face is tightened and seems nervous and hesitating. If you create an overview on this individual's cold reading, you will clearly notice certain contradictions between the serious / bleak side of the picture that emanates from him and his hesitating body language that discloses a lack of confidence in him.
Here are some points to perpetuate through cold reading:

First, do not perceive a prior idea on what his interlocutor could look like in order to avoid surprises and thus influence your brain especially if that is exactly what that he is waiting for.

Second, examine his appearance, his visual communication. This is not about determining if his watch is a Rolex or a" useless gadget " but in discerning his visual impact that is presented to those around him. What impression does your interlocutor give you? Believe me, your brain has already captured this image and gained an idea about it. Otherwise, advertising would not prevail any longer.

Third, resolve on your interlocutor's background and the personal situation. They may only be theories but believe me, not only will this reflection become heightened given the time and experience but in addition, you will progressively be doing the exact thing needed. This can avoid you breaking into several surprises.

Fourth, observe his body movements. This will consent you to confront him directly, along with the previous visual impact analysis and thus, determine whether this visual communication is voluntary or not. This analysis will provide you with an idea on the protagonist's disposition and anticipate on the flow of events.

Let us rewind this movie a little and imagine that you do not do any cold reading and therefore you wouldn't be concerned on any of the four points above.

The meeting is about to begin, and the protagonists had not yet arrived and you think, seen the context of the situation (the dismissals and the environmental stress that reigns in the premises) that the investors will look like men in black, dark glasses, black FBI cars, shortly, like some insensible and merciless people. And then you see this good old gentleman in a white shirt, gray hair, small glasses and all in smiles, entering the room. Then, you glance at the second investor in a complete black suit. Hence, immediately, you will remain focused on this very appeasing gentleman who adds in a few colors and keeps smiling in this gloomy atmosphere. This image is imprinted in your brain and in that of your associates. What is risking here, is that all the questions, discussions, are about to be directed towards this gentleman who is indeed the most experienced !

What really happened, during this meeting, was that most of the perceptible questions were directed to the youngest man since cold reading lead the way in determining what the weak point in this meeting was. These questions, presently forwarded to this man, made him even more embarrassed than at first. He had difficulties in answering it correctly and was almost reprimanded the whole time by his experienced associate. We have succeeded in incorporating a particular disrepute to the meeting.

You had already noticed this, cold reading can effectively contribute in detecting weak points in a situation and consequently, lead an attack.

In order to instigate an improvement in your potential of cold reading, you can practice it on your interlocutors. Once this becomes a habit, then try, (even if you might not be in any precise background such as reflection imprints related to the pleasant gentleman; his age, its experience) to understand your interlocutor's personality. Doing this exercise will only accustom you to think in this manner. Then practice examining the body language of people with whom you talk or even on those who you can observe daily.

Let us inquire into an example, of a woman who is to be interviewed on a big American television channel. This lady's involvement is eagerly expected since the concern for which she appears is very mediatized and divisive.

Let us review the four elements contributing to a compelling cold reading: do not try to guess what the person might look like or his appearance if we have already seen him. Analyse his visual impact, contemplate on his background and examine his body language.

The interview begins. While the journalist revises on certain facts for the TV viewers, the camera is directed towards this woman for around thirty seconds. She is dressed in a white colored pair of trousers with a matching white sleeveless top and a small, almost whitish green colored woolen cardigan. She is neither wearing a watch, nor any jewelry.
No necklaces, earrings or even rings, absolutely nothing. This woman conveys an impression of simplicity, relaxation and openness. The cardigan is opened conveying the following oblivious image: I am opened to you and you can also ask me any desired questions.

Analysis and opinion on the background related to this person.

This person is eagerly expected by the media. She divides the opinion, and her words and the image she releases, will also be very important. When you have to appear at a job interview would you go in a tracksuit? Of course not ,since you are aware that you'll be observed. The same principle applies here. The point that seems totally unbelievable is the complete lack of jewelry. A majority of women (at least all those whom I know) wear jewelry under all conditions. Not necessarily, as much as Mister T but at least a small jewel. These details persuade me to think that the clothing appearance of this woman was prepared and I shall say even recommended, to create a pleasant and relaxed visual impact that your brain has captured well.

With respect to her behavioural analysis. This woman is seated on a chair, with joint hands, as if one over the other and all lying on her legs. I made a reference to this position previously during the example where the person keeps standing in a public transport.

Joint hands securing privacy, creating a defense. This woman has the same but seated posture. This reveals a certain stress. Relatively difficult to discern if this person is hiding something, for who would really feel at ease in front of cameras, journalistic questions and being watched by millions of people. It is quite later that gestures will be determining the discrepancy between her words and her actual thoughts.

In summing up this cold reading, we notice that the image rendered by this woman is contradicted through her gestures. This will lead to reinforce the theory of visual impact analysis and the background in order to fathom out the voluntary communication of an image.

Thus, the more you stare, the more faster you will be capable of executing this cold reading. Precisely, within a few seconds.

Here is to summarize the four essential points for an effective cold reading.

1) Do not try to postulate how the person you are about to meet, will look like. If this person tries to attract you into his game by setting up his visual aspect, it would be better not to have too much of a discrepancy between your perceived idea and the reality. Contrast is important as much as surprise, and therefore, the impression in your brain is also significant as much as emotion. Feelings have a very strong connection with the memory process. Bear in mind, that your brain will capture whatever it sees within seconds.

2) A visual Analysis of your interlocutor. It allows you to determine the visual impact and whether the person deliberately wants to exploit the other. It allows you to become more conscious of yourself.

3) An opinion on the personal background of the person.

4) Behavioral Analysis of the person.

The last three points discussed above will benefit you with some consequential indications about the person in front of you. A clear judgment on his disposition can be made through this and thus, you may choose to "attack "this person with a better approach or, anticipate his reactions, if in case, you have no initiative. Along with an effective training, you could almost persuade others that you are competent in reading their thoughts.

But this is a strategy used in mentalism, isn't it?

The first point, lays the foundation for what we will be elaborating in the next chapters. Specifically, a mentalism technique known as "misdirection" or, to be more accurate: "the misappropriation of attention". These can be extremely intimidating for professional liars. You have just witnessed a similar example during the first investor's story.

In the next chapter, we will explore a cold reading technique commonly used by psychics, mentalists, particularly during magic tricks, and in addition by sales representatives or swindlers. Certain people do this unconsciously but others carefully scrutinize on the techniques, that we are about to see in depth.

Welcome to the frosty world of cold reading...
Sorry for this joke.

Chapter 4

<u>COLD and</u>
<u>CONSTANT READING</u>

Throughout the previous chapter, I intentionally disregarded the distinction between the terms "cold reading" (lecture à froid in French) which symbolizes my technique of determining the body language, and "cold reading" which we will be investigating and which is, in my point of view, a true art form.

What is cold reading?

Cold Reading is a successful blend of manipulation techniques, psychological knowledge of the human and all other perceptions surrounded by statistical knowledge of everyone's habits.
These three parameters when considered together, along with the addition of some several other additional parameters, empowers in acquiring a set of very impressive manipulation results. These techniques are practiced in mentalism, magic, communication and further allows to determine another's body language. This determination leads towards practices such as foresight, mediumship and all other areas where logic reaches its extremities.

Clairvoyance is the art to perceive information by using flashes, mental images, sensations from the past, present or future events. A psychic is a person with the proficiency to become a communication channel between the spiritual world and ours. This is entirely similar to Patrick Jane from the TV series 'The Mentalist'. Before serving the police, the hero in the series was a psychic and was capable of communicating with dead people. He made his living by arranging collective sessions where he could communicate with the dead.

There are at present, actual people who do this and make their living extremely well through this. The field of psychics is a real industry based on billions of earnings generated each year. The clairvoyance industry is one part of this which can be easily found on the Internet, TV, "psychological" newspapers that simply misemploys innocent people with personal difficulties in a shameful way.

I am now about to dive into the depths of this art since I believe that this is the most accomplished, with regard to cold reading.

Besides my examples, I rendered two other telephone consultations, broadcasted live on TV. These are two very good cold reading examples. Certain clairvoyants / psychics attending these broadcasts do not hesitate to reply yes to your questions whatever they may be, even before you finished asking, by randomly spinning two or three cards.

This is solely done, under the guise of their reputation in the field. But how do they earn this reputation? How do their predictions always seem to come true? It is naturally the testimonies of people that often certify their reputations and you will notice what psychics actually consider in their visions through both the examples; we are now about to examine. Apart from this, there are plenty of examples about people wasting several thousand dollars for these consultations. Not very long ago, a friend with whom I exchange views on almost everything, shared with me, a consultation that she had with a psychic a few days ago.

After her narration concluded, I debunked all what the psychic had revealed to her, point by point with great ease (and with her permission, of course).

You will also have the opportunity of doing so, by the end of this chapter and with the same ease. I shall show you through A + B how the reputation of such people is created and thus, their credibility as well.

I would like to introduce, Pierre. He is a psychic and a friend with whom I am acquainted for more than fifteen years now. I met him at a fitness gym, where I used to work as a sports trainer at the time, via a common friend who used to come regularly to train with him.

One day while we were discussing about psychic powers, she offered to introduce me to him. He does not do this as his job, nor does he earn any income with this gift and practices it only on his close friends. On the other hand, he reveals a number of surprising predictions through the interpretation of cards and even speaks from time to time about visual flashes based on specific events.

Having empathize with him and in return for the numerous advise that I had lavished on him regarding sports, he suggested a session, in order to question my skepticism concerning clairvoyance.

I am going to render to you more or less on what he narrated to me at the time. This really happened fifteen years ago but I had taken down some notes that I had carefully preserved (yes, I note down and always preserve whatever is in my interests). Therefore, take down notes and memorize these dialogues for we shall analyze them farther in this chapter.

Let's start: *"So, Philippe, I see in you; a serious, determined person who always strive to attain his objectives. But there is always an interest behind all this; you are not the kind to do things without any purpose. You don't like wasting time. I also see in you, someone opened to others. People do not waver to confide in you. "*

Since there wasn't any such topic that I wished to tackle with him, he suggested to discuss regarding jobs and affairs. Ah well, yes! Let's start: *" I see what you will be doing in the future as a job, a very good career, you will give way to it and occupy with rewarding functions (he knew that I was to enter the Police soon). But I also see that you will be engaging in something new, though I am unable to see what that is, it is something which perhaps, does not yet exist. Maybe something related to technology. "*

Hum…. well all right, I said to myself, but what about affairs? I passed over all the conditions and procedures that include in setting up the session such as, concentrating, reading cards, thinking, interpreting etc.

Answer: " *ah, as for this I perceived a particularly clear image, and the interpretation of cards testify this further, this is dealing with the girl you have just met, I see a rather strong relationship with regard to money and I do not see anything necessarily sustainable in this relationship. I think that you should be more concerned about this.*"

Ah, it is certainly not very pleasing to hear such things. And yet, everything did go smoothly a several months later, she indeed had a certain interest for money. Damned! But he was right. Thus, he really was gifted.

And if I tell you that, in fact, he has no gift, and that everything he disclosed to me was only a series of sentences based on some readings from your humble servant? I was partially subjected to cold-reading. Yes, I declare to you, that all this is solely a matter of cold-reading and a manipulation of information.
But what about the flash that he had about my girlfriend? How did he do that?

Let's come back to the present. Having worked for several weeks on cold reading and gaining an intensive training in the art of clairvoyance together with Pierre, he challenged me, precisely, my experience in lie detection, to prove that the flashes that he would have on a friend with whom he had already scheduled a session, were false. Hum.., I am willing to moonwalk all around the world, if ever I fail in that area.
After a brief telephone conversation with Anne during which, she inquired me for my birth date and where I live, I agreed upon an hour and a place for the consultation. The meeting will be held at her place since it was where she usually receives her customers.
After drawing out cards and an overall description of my

personality is given, similar to the interview held with Pierre, she asked me on what topic, I wanted to address before speaking about the visions that she had. Then, I asked her to disclose to me about my future profession.

Let us begin: *"I see an interesting, fascinating job but I also see an evolution in this job, that persists to be quite distorted but I shall say that within about three to six months, there are signs of a possible improvement. Either you swap out of the frame, or progress within the company.*
I perceive a name, Eric or Frédéric. Are you familiar with one of these names? "
Surprisingly, yes, there is an Eric, my project director AND Frédéric! Having mentioned this to her, I saw her smile slightly for a second. She affirmed me that this Eric could have something in particular with my future profession. Next, she moved on to the visions that she had. Visions that she generally has at the very first sight of a person.

Here are her remarks: *"I had a vision of a car crash, nothing serious other than a few damages. I didn't see any date and I am unable to say when this could happen. But the strongest and the continually lingering vision in my mind, is the presence of the numbers 6432 or 6435 closely related to you.*

There is something that you possess relating to this number, I am sure, for it was a really clear flash. How did you come? Walking? By bus or car? "

In an airplane, I tell her (no, I am just joking, by car).
The session concluded. While I was getting ready to leave, Anne says: *"I will be having an interval of about thirty minutes, since my next customer will not be coming till then, so, may I accompany you and see your car, if you allow me to? "*

Yes, I had no problem in unveiling cold reading during the course of the session; I confess that I was shocked, there. Since along the path leading to my car, accompanied with Anne, I wondered about these numbers and their relationship with me, like a silly man. Which was, I suddenly remembered, being in front of my car, the first number on my license plate.

" OK, this is exactly the number; I had seen in my flash, I wasn't sure it had anything to do with your car, thank you." Anne tells me with the smile.

Hmmm.. But how did she know? yet, I didn't notice anyone coming on the street and her clairvoyance office is on a building at the back of a courtyard.
Would she be having a true gift? You shall encounter the answer a little farther in this chapter, but in the meantime...

Here is the further progress of the chapter.

I would like to present to you the transcription of a television program where viewers can call the psychics available on the screen and ask them a question. Feel free to have the liberty of reading this dialogue since we will analyse it and begin to deal with cold reading afterwards. Next, I shall present to you another dialogue in this show so that you can practice. Dialogues are transcribed as they were articulated, only the names are altered.

Dialogue1

Patricia, the psychic / medium, is seated alongside the presenter who welcomes the clients. The presenter asks Patricia how she arrives into predictions. She explains to him, that it is done while listening to the client's voice where she collects vibrations and images that she then interprets.

The presenter receives a call: "we will welcome Lucienne, hello

Lucienne

-
  Hello; yes I am Lucienne from Vendée (east of France).
- *Hello Lucienne, How are you?*

- *I am feeling fine, just like beautiful bright sun.*

- *Well, this is your chance to ask your question from our medium Patricia.*

- *All right, hello Patricia "*

- *Thus, medium Patricia speaks: " hello Lucienne, I have no idea but why do I have the impression that I already know you.*

- *Euh (Lucienne thinks about a good moment), well, I don't really know.*

- *All right, it must be a mistake then, could you give me your age, Lucienne?*

- *I just became 68, this May.*

- *68?! But what form, right!*

- *Euh, not always.*

- *No, but the morale is good, but however, I do see a lot of energy in you.*

- *That's true.*

- *Well, Lucienne you should not be busy with too many people around you since I believe that you have a notion of giving too much.*

- *Indeed.*

- *You need to be more concerned about you. Let's start; I*

will listen to your question.

- *Hence, I intend to sell my apartment in the near future, do you happen to see me moving into an apartment with someone or not?*

- *About to sell your apartment (psychic's thought) it's not on sale, is it?*

- *No, I plan to sell it within the next year.*

- *(The psychic contemplates for a few seconds) so, this is an apartment that can be sold easily since its location is good. (The sentence sounds like a question)*

- *Yes.*

- *(The psychic replies immediately) euh……. it's not too high. (The sentence still rings like a question)*

- *No, it's in the ground floor.*

- *Ah of course, there you are, I saw it wasn't too high. (Voluntary silence)*

- *Do you see me moving into another apartment with someone in the future?*

- *Euh, why I have Michel, who is Michel?*

- *Ah I don't know.*

- *Since at the moment, there is really no one in your life. (As a question)*

- *Yes, Patrick is there.*

- *Patrick... Oh isn't he a little reluctant?*

- *Euh yes, just a little. "*

- *The presenter interrupts by saying that this is perhaps a future encounter. The medium takes over: "In my viewpoint, I sense Patrick to be reluctant.*

- *Do you need his birth date (pursues Lucienne)?*

- *No, but I perceive that he is younger.*

- *Euh, thirteen years younger than me.*

- *Ah! Listen, there is some understanding between you, something that is constructive but in order to live together, I feel, there is something lacking. But Lucienne, I can answer you very clearly.*

- *Let's proceed.*

- *You will move, that's for sure, I am not sure if it'll be with your Patrick but however I am in the opinion that you may have someone. At the moment, perhaps, you might not know him. But, to me, it's someone who seems to be Michel or Jean-Michel who is really good. You might come across him right under your nose, in a shopping mall or somewhere like that for I see something that stretches out, somewhere, where shopping is done. But Patrick, I don't know, to me, he seems to be a little reluctant, and I can't say if he is still ready to move.*

- *At the moment he is in a flat share.*

- *Yes, but I can't say if he is ready to change his life so suddenly, in order to move, but nevertheless, you will move. If it's with him, so much the better Lucienne, but I have the impression that it could be with somebody else.*

- *(Lucienne's thought)*

- *But this Patrick, he is kind....*

- *Oh my god.*

- *He is someone who is always left spoiled by everyone.*

- *Entirely.*

- *He has lost a lot, he has already lost a situation.*

- *Yes, he is currently working.*

- *Yes, but he has been cutting his work, he is detained there, but he has plenty of determinations in his mind.*

- *Exactly, he is in a flat share but he once told me "I wish to take over my freedom ".*

- *Yes ,but to take over his freedom, he won't be taking it at once since he lacks money, he has no intention to end up with nothing.*

- *Absolutely. (Continues Lucienne)*

- *And to buy a big apartment, even if you give him everything, and if you wish to share everything with him he is not someone who would be too willing to fight for. He is quite proud. Without that, your relationship with him would have been already more lasting.*

- *I agree.*

- *In addition, he wants to mark his territory.*

- *Exactly.*

- *Patrick is adorable, and a very kind person. (The psychic moves on)*

- *Oh my god, his sign is Virgo.*

- *Well, I will state why not Patrick, but you will meet someone who has nothing to do with Patrick. Your house will be sold in a good condition to sell, it's situated well, so, here we are. (Forced silence)*

- *I don't have to wait any longer then?*

- *Well, I don't like people continuing to keep on waiting since fate is always fate. But anyway, I think, you are left with only that at present(quite answers Lucienne at the same time). Here we are, yet this is going in the right direction, but Patrick, he is not yet ready to leave what he has. He is willing to, but he also wants to regain some financial strength.*

- *I believe this will perhaps be over at the end of the year, or the beginning of the other (questions Lucienne)?*

- *Euh yes, I think so, since I also see that he has debts.*

- *Euh oh yes! It's true, yes. I hope that he will be standing on his feet by the next year.*

- *Bear in mind, that if you are inclined to help him, he will accept it but I am reminding you that he also wishes to earn something on his own, and reattain self-confidence in him and thus, that's what's most important. (Lucienne says nothing) Lucienne?*

- *He will regain his self-confidence next year then.*

- *Yes and I believe, you can help him as well. There are feelings with regard to this.*

- *On Both sides?*

- *Yes but he is not used to showing his feelings, he is someone who is a little introvert*

- *Entirely. "*

Thus, Lucienne moves on to the presenter." Well, I appreciate for all that you have said "says Lucienne. The dialogue concludes.

Here are four significant elements that is a part of the manipulation process which would be beneficial if taken into consideration.

The first point is the disposition of the person who is about to consult a psychic. It could be someone with a traumatic period in his life. He could be desperate, undecided, and anguished. He needs to take an important decision in his life but is clueless; he is petrified on what the future could bring to him or to his close relations. Shortly, all the anxieties in life for which it is normal to fret and would prefer to be answered. Who would not have had a bad move in his life? Some people seems to be more resistant to the stress than others. Others can be a little more vulnerable. And I wish somebody knew the answers to my questions? At least my friends? No, not any more, for they have their own concerns. My neighbors? My parents? It is during these difficult times, these moments of doubts that we would prefer to have an indication on what our future would encounter to us. The person that I have just met, is she someone I can confide in? Am I going to continue my life with her? I must move to another district for my work. I will have to move with my whole family. Or should I resign? What would be the best decision to take? And what if I consulted a psychic?
This first point has a noteworthy importance; it is the state of expectancy that is present in the "customer". This will vastly contribute to a better progress in the session.

The second point.

Neutralize the customer's analyzing and thinking potential by using the technique that makes the customer realize that visions, flashes, and sensations that are perceived, are not necessarily precise. And especially, that these visions are only the interpretation of something, in this case it would be: cards which were drawn out. Thus, this is not necessary for the psychic, unless satisfactory results are not achieved. It is only an additional measure to obtain the customer's cooperation unintentionally. The customer being in a state of expectancy will do anything under his power to look for the slightest correspondence in his life. And you will notice the swirl used by these psychics when the customer finds nothing in relation to an element of his life. Once this simple cooperation is acquired, the door is wide open for predictions such as: "I *see a certain Eric in your life or a Frédéric who seems to have a something in common with the question that you put forward. Do you happen to know an Eric or a Frédéric?*

- *Euh not, not really.*

- *Look very well for maybe a Cédric.*

- *I know an Erica on the contrary...*

- *That's right! "*

Even though you will not find any first name or surname closely or remotely connected to Eric, the psychic will certainly answer you with an unbound assurance: *"well, don't forget to keep this first name in mind, for you will certainly meet a person with the consonance "Eric " who will be related to your business »*

Et voila.

The second point is hence important; to deport the psychic's power with the interpretation of cards or other measures, on visions, flashes etc. This will contribute in not directly laying hold on the psychic since he is only interpreting whatever he sees or perceives.

The customer is in such a state of expectancy for answers where he will also create in him an accidental state of cooperativeness. Poor psychic, this power must be hard for him, if only I can help him interpret... the client may think.

Generally, from the beginning of the interview, the psychic will enlighten you about his working procedure. Some may mix tactile contacts such as touching hands in order to pretend the emergence of flashes, then reading cards, doing a little numerology, and then finally delivering their interpretations to you.

The third point.

In my cold reading method, I embarked on an extremely important point about visual impact; the voluntary transmission of an image to the other. If the dress style of a psychic passes on a certain professional image of his job, thus creating a suitable atmosphere, is also quite important. The atmosphere in which you are welcomed, depends obviously on the psychic but generally the way you experience a particular atmosphere once you enter a church or a court, is similar to what you will feel once you enter a clairvoyance office. The customer needs to feel welcome in one's home since it has a slight effect in making the customer feel privileged or grateful for becoming a little intimate with the psychic. It can even contribute to strengthen his confidence.

The fourth point.

A little contemplation shows that, all our measures and acts seem to be motivated by the desire in wanting to eradicate pain or look for happiness. Would you be more inclined for good or evil? Would you be more inclined for happiness or pain? Would you be more inclined for things that are well or things that go badly? If you associate these to the customer's strong state of expectancy, there will be an interesting phenomenon. This one will have a strong tendency to hold on only what interests him. And thus, to only hold on to those interpretations and predictions that will exactly affect him. And forget the rest. If the psychic always ensures not to offend you and only predict things that goes in the right direction, or on your behalf, then, the mere fact where you assumed that his predictions are not directly provided by him but that he is only interpreting signs, the failures will be simply disregarded and will be forgotten very fast. This phenomenon contributes to a great extent in creating a reputation for the psychic / medium.

Before analyzing the dialogue above, let us recapitulate four important points:

1) The atmosphere created by the psychic/ medium.

2) The state of expectancy of the person coming to consult.

3) The psychic explaining to the customer that he interprets signs, images, flashes, and that they will perhaps, not be precise. This obliviously occurs to the customer's mind, the idea that he will be able to « help » the psychic with his interpretations. This has the effect of obstructing the customer's analyzing attempts.

4) The customer's state of expectation will make him remember only those predictions that affect him and thus, forget the rest.

Let us decipher this telephone and broadcast session.

Firstly, the atmosphere. If there is no atmosphere with a special room prepared to conduct the clairvoyance, here, it is a television studio. It could have a chilling effect for those who don't prefer spreading out in public. However, there are matters to analysis and especially regarding displayed images. This is a television program so it is something important. And if this is something important then, the psychics/ mediums that get involved in this broadcast, are all reputed. Besides, many people who call up to have an interview with them think that they must be effective.

In any case, psychics who work for these television programs are introduced as renowned psychics who practice psychology as their job. Subsequently, at the beginning of the program, the presenter always requests the psychic to briefly explain how he works. Is it with cards, does he have flashes when he hears someone's voice or when he looks at his photo? It is at this moment that you become aware that the psychic is only interpreting something, and he cannot even see predictions. Even if he has a flash, he will always remember to tell you something like "I see an image, I feel something, I perceive".
When the session begins, the psychic will always ask you when the last time you consulted a psychic / medium was. You might think that in this world of outstanding psychic powers, interference could take place between mediums.

Well no. For a very simple reason.
In our example where the psychic practices her consultancy via a telephone, hence, she cannot see the person, this is why she says: "I don't know why, but I have the impression that I know you ". The customer dashes with her eyes closed: " no, possibly last year ". This avoids the psychic from rendering a second prediction for someone she had recently already conducted a session and hence, prevents her from predicting something else, perhaps even the opposite of what she had told her before.

That is why, even during a private session, a psychic will always ask you for this, in order to avoid saying the opposite of what one of her colleagues would have told you, in case you decided to consult several psychics. That is why they also advise you to consult a psychic every three to six months, for an instance. In our broadcasting example, the psychic, not being able to see her interlocutor, certainly won't want to speak again with the same person.

A person with psychological powers should already be aware on why you are there, what must be the purpose of your visit, isn't it? Without asking you the question. It is possible to do so with triumph, given a considerable amount of experience on cold reading; in fact, there are psychics who don't even care! In this broadcast, viewers are invited, certainly before beginning the program, so as to give their age and residency as soon as they are introduced to the psychics. These are two consequential indications that must be revealed before starting to spin some initial predictions or play on some particular points related to these areas, etc. Age plays a vital role in cold reading, it is considered to be one of the statistical elements that succeed in rendering some of the most indications about a person.

As a matter of fact, the various phases that we go through in life coincide with distinct age brackets. Adolescence is categorized for those between 14 to 18 years, the gateway to working life extends from 18 to 25 years, creating a family, marriage, and children comes between 20 to 35 years. And, between 35 to 45 years; several transitions in life may occur, such as separation, divorce and career counseling. On the edge of about fifty, an emotional evolution and a number of other issues begin to arise, particularly, about future, health, or death. These are only majorities and need not necessarily correspond to everyone but once these age brackets are incorporated with three reasonable factors as to why people tend to confide in psychics; you may hence, gain a better conception regarding why they are there.

Three main factors that persuade people to consult psychics are:
- relationships / sex
- money / career
- health

Anne gave me the following statistics derived directly from her consultations. Customarily, young people of roughly about 20-25 years, who come to her, had especially sought out for consultations regarding romantic stories. They were mostly men.

But the critical elements among her customers are mostly women, nearly 30 % from 30 to 35 years old, 30 % of more than 40 years and 40 % of more than fifty years. Almost all the problems of her customers who are around thirty are: either single women who wonder if they will soon meet someone special (No. 1, relationships), or women already in a relationship wondering if their relationship will last any longer. Also, there may be issues relating to work, a new job or a change of company.

In the category of women of more than forty years; the problems are always regarding relationships / sex, but more focused on questions based on divorce, calling the couple to be questioned or potential relocation.

Women of more than fifty years also dread with concern to relationships that they carry on with a man. If they are single, their doubts would be the anxiety of putting an end to being alone. Sometimes, these are male customers of about forty years but their issues always end up with regard to work.

Hence, it is determined that these brief statistics correspond to the three factors mentioned above. Least concerns are with regard to health even though she has already received several people wondering about the health of a loved one.

This equation which integrates relationships, work, health and the age category of people lays the foundation for cold reading. You can further add to this equation; the customer's disposition, which in other words defines; his state of expectancy, his cooperative state (we discerned why) and the fact that he will only hold onto the positive points or be well-focused on the psychic.

Let us proceed with the analysis of the dialogue.

Having used the technique of time that allows her to verify if she had recently consulted this person; Patricia, the psychic, asks for Lucienne's age! Was she unable to guess it? Of course not, just to ask for it. Besides, this will allow Patricia to tighten her grip regarding Lucienne's potential problem. Lucienne had also given her residency, when she introduced herself. "68 years" says Lucienne in a quite spirited way that Patricia immediately used and said: "68? But what an energy!"
Immediately opposed to this by Lucienne with a" no, not really ". How does Patricia revive? " No, but the morale is good, but however, I do see a lot of energy in you."
The slightest indication can be thus applied, to the sound and the energetic tone of Lucienne's voice here. Has Patricia made a mistake? Not a very serious one though, "however, I do see a lot of energy in you " is a common phrase that is always adopted.
Are you energetic? Good! Then she is right, since this will always be a compliment that will please you (always go in the right direction) and can be used later by mentioning it, acting like a psychic who has very well identified you.
" Well, Lucienne you should not be busy with too many people around you since I believe that you have a notion of giving too much ".
This is further confirmed by Lucienne. It is a common aspect where everyone has already spent or given too much for something or somebody, for some work but often have not been rewarded for what it's worth, isn't it? Even if it had happened ten years ago for you, you will still remember as you recall the past (cooperation with the clairvoyant). Therefore, there aren't many risks of saying this phrase. If at least for once, this becomes true, then she will earn a point, otherwise you will merely forget it very soon and will rather concentrate on the progress of the interview.
Since the only thing that interests you is actually; the answer to your question.

During the interview, rather than guess or feel what will be the question, Patricia directly puts forward the question! "Let's start Lucienne, what is your question? ".

What ?! A little easy don't you think ? What a shame. Patricia now has all the elements in hand; residency, age and the reason she called! What more is left to build up a comprehensive and complete scenario, I ask you. This is how certain so-called renowned psychics do not even make the simplest effort but just answer: "yes, it's good that this will happen, might take some time but I see that you are someone patient".

This psychic, Patricia is trying to render a clairvoyance impression by using several techniques that we will be exploring farther.
Lucienne wishes to know, if she is going to move into an apartment with someone and Patricia is about to use the double sided question technique, which is capable of covering both answer options. Example: "Your apartment is not on sale, is it?" As you will have understood it, this phrase contributes in answering to both the possible answers. Firstly, an assumption is released (it's not on sale) next, a substantiation (is it?). In any case, however, Patricia succeeds to hit the target. By leaving a pause between the first assumption and its opposite, Patricia lets believe that she had a vision in the meantime and may thus switch from one to the other. "so, this is an apartment that can be sold easily since its location is good ".

If someone asked you to select a number from 1 to 100, where would you place your finger to have most of the luck in gaining success? In the middle. This is the balance technique that will save you from taking too many risks. Therefore, in a 10-storeyed building, an apartment which is not too high fits perfectly. Neither too high nor too low.

The affirmative phrase "it's not too high." rings as a matter of fact, like a question according to Patricia's tone. **But if in addition, you add the word "high" and the negation " is not " then the question can be interpreted as: "it's not placed too high, is it?".**

This is a tricky method of hiding the double sided technique which we have just indicated.

" Ah of course, there you are, I saw it wasn't too high" answers Patricia to Lucienne who has just told her that her apartment is in the ground floor.

Lucienne continues by raising the question: "Do you see me moving into another apartment with someone in the future? ". Patricia will now use a technique where some nonsense is spoken along with a certain chance of success at the same time, like: " Euh, why I have Michel, who is Michel?" There is however, a slight cleverness used here. Let us imagine that Patricia answered: "I see a name that begins with an M, do you know anyone who has a name beginning with an M? ".

Statistically, there could be a number of names starting with an M. Moreover, there may even be some strong chances where you know or knew a name with an M. If that becomes the case, then the psychic will respond: "well, you might have to deal with this M. ".

Why does Patricia reduce her chances by giving a whole name? Having said in a confident and assured way by interrupting Lucienne; "why I have Michel?" will appear more bold and certain. Moreover, you will affirm yourself that she would not take the risk of collapsing live in front of you and think that this name must be holding some importance, even if you did not know who Michel was.

The psychic will ask you to look deeper and if you still fail to find it, then she will tell you: "well, listen to me, I see this Michel, he will certainly meet you and he is someone significantly related to your business, remember this well."

Now, imagine that she was really successful, and you know Michel. What a vision! She had really hit the mark, I know Michel really well, she is indeed talented!

This is how reputation is created. Let us put this conversation aside for a while in order to examine the question.

Let us say that there might be a one-in-ten chance, that my customer knows Michel. Nine out of ten, that I will make a mistake and give you an evasive sentence like the example we just saw. But one out of ten that I will hit it and impress you. And it is this impressed person who will gladly leave a recommendation on the psychic's website. It is this person who will spread the word about this psychic's extraordinary abilities. You may not attend clairvoyance sessions that are of no interest to you, and you will neither consult a psychic who has already made nine out of ten mistakes. On the other hand, you will certainly view **all** the "great" comments that have been left for "a one-in-ten person" whose predictions had turned out just right. I am only speaking about 'the name Michel example' but this entirely applies to all the predictions that will be made for you in the coming six months.

Alright, I am going to make a prediction for you: " I see, by the end of the year, in December, perhaps by the 20th or a quite closer date, a significant event coming up for you. You will meet a woman; she is wearing glasses and will be related to this event. "

Here is a comprehensive example on a prediction that could be made for you. It looks precise, yet, if we analyze it, there is a high likelihood of achieving it. For example, you expect it to happen on the 20th, and there can be lots of things happening on one single day, you may go Christmas shopping and meet people, you will perhaps hear news of someone who you had not seen for a long time. If it's not 20th, it will be a quite closer date; this leaves a margin of about ten days until you really meet this woman. This woman can be your neighbor, a friend who wears glasses, an office friend, the doctor or even the post woman. It can be during a birthday, Christmas holidays, shortly, there are in fact, plenty of possibilities. In addition, the psychic will give you a considerably far off date, like; three to six months, so you won't remember about this session any further.

However, if this F.P.F.L.S. (False prediction for a high likelihood of success) hits the target, then, this will retain in your mind for a long time and you will further recommend me to everyone else interested.

If I manage to hit about ten times in this way, it will benefit me with a good showcase of comments along with an excellent reputation, don't you think?
Let us return to the dialogue.

> Patricia has just declared: " *why I have Michel, who is Michel?* "
- *I don't know.*

- *Since at the moment, there is really no one in your life.*

- *Yes, Patrick is there.*

- *Patrick... Oh isn't he a little reluctant?*

- *Euh yes, just a little. "*

How does Patricia perceive that Patrick is reluctant? This is also an art of cold reading; notice well, remember and analyze correctly of what your customer has stated.

The question that Lucienne asks at the beginning, thus, renders many indications: " Hence, I intend to sell my apartment in the near future, do you happen to see me moving into an apartment with someone or not?"

The indications are:

1) Moving into an apartment?

2) With someone?

3) Sell?

4) In the near future?

If Patricia used a double sided question (" your apartment, it's not still on sale, is it? ")and the words used by Lucienne ("No, I plan to sell it within the next year ") leads to confirm along with some strong chances of success that the apartment is not still for sale. Therefore it is necessary, to analyze the sentence in order to determine if it contains any more indications than it appears to have.

The part of the sentence: " you happen to see me moving into an apartment with someone or not " is doubtful. If Lucienne did not have anyone special in her life, she would have simply asked if she was going to meet someone or if she was simply moving.

 Thus, this articulation, suspects the presence of a man. And if Lucienne is here, it is only because she wants to ask a question, since she has a problem, which must definitely be related to this man and to the fact of moving with him. Two questions can be put forward, that makes Patricia more cautious: "there is really no one in your life? ". The word actually supposes that there could be someone in Lucienne's life but she is perhaps not very attached to him. You could even take a risk and increase your chances of further heightening your reputation by saying: "I see that you have somebody in your life "along with a good chance of success. There would be hence, a problem of moving with someone and therefore, it is a good chance that there is reluctance on one side or the other among the protagonists.

How can we determine if it is Lucienne who is reluctant or this man named Patrick? The rare books specialized on cold reading draw up a list of general behavioral patterns in men and women with their own differences. It further includes some of the intrinsic fears in men and women. One of the fears in men is commitment. Here, with respect to Lucienne, there is a question of moving with a man, thus, the psychic may come up with the assumption that Patrick might be reluctant. If in case, the psychic makes a mistake, she can always get back on her feet after the swirl: "This is strange, I perceive that he is however, a little reluctant, did he not speak to you about it? "

Given that this is about his feelings, which are invisible things, it is thus, difficult to discern what exactly takes place in Patrick's head. Therefore, it will always be difficult for Lucienne to verify.

Let us resume once more. The medium continues: " In my viewpoint, I sense Patrick to be reluctant. Perhaps, he might also be longing, but he is reluctant ".

This is a double sided sentence, he is reluctant but he is also perhaps longing.

"I perceive that he is younger" declares the psychic. This is quite a risky assertion than the rest. But if we consider that this has a one-in-two chance to succeed, and that he can very well be a year younger, or a few months; this heightens the possibilities. Otherwise she can always answer that she sees him younger at heart, that he is physically young for example, like practicing some sport, but in this case of course, she succeeds. Patricia certainly scored points in the eyes of Lucienne.

Patricia further continues: " You will move, that's for sure; I am not sure if it'll be with your Patrick but however I am in the opinion that you may have someone. At the moment, perhaps, you might not know him. But, to me, it's someone who seems to be Michel or Jean-Michel who is really good. You might come across him right under your nose, in a shopping mall or somewhere like that for I see something that stretches out, somewhere, where shopping is done. But Patrick, I don't know, to me, he seems to be a little reluctant, and I can't say if he is still ready to move."

The psychic returns to her so-called vision of the well-known Michel but tries to broaden the scope with a Jean-Michel. I confer you that the typical meeting place is: the shopping mall.

What is the most likely method to succeed? Where most unknowns are met: the shopping mall! This meeting may fall on you without warning, and if you miss it by chance, it will entirely be your fault, for you had not looked enough for Jean-Michel in this shopping mall !

Patricia insists that Lucienne will move. Actually, she said this verbally, and hence, from the likelihood of probability, the risk of failing is low. Especially as this is about selling an apartment (it is Lucienne who said it!) which is not the same approach she would take if she was a tenant. Therefore, this is certainly a carefully considered decision on behalf of Lucienne. In fact Lucienne's real question is to know if it will be with Patrick or not. This being made quite clear, the psychic changes the subject again. Did you notice how Patricia, the psychic makes use of all the information that she has? And Lucienne was willing to provide her some more information with which Patricia was ready to play: "at the moment he is in a flat share."
And what an information! In fact, a series of information. Lucienne is 68 years old and Patrick being 13 less, must be 55 years. Being in a flat share at this age means a whole life trajectory having subjected to some sudden accidents such as a

divorce for instance or perhaps a job loss; but this implies a high likelihood that Patrick's financial situation is not so good. The psychic will manipulate this information but neither at once nor directly. Simply imagine that after Lucienne's disclosure, you interfere by saying: "I see that the financial situation of Patrick is not very good ". It would seem too obvious. No, instead of this Patricia continues to express on moving again, that it is not bound to happen with Patrick. Then she moves on with: "he is a kind person Patrick..."

Lucienne's answer is: " oh, my god ". The way Lucienne pronounces these words interprets a certain exhaustion. An exhaustion that probably implies that Patrick is someone too kind. The psychic may thus announce in order to meddle too much; that he is someone who was always left "spoiled" by everyone. This is confirmed by Lucienne. Now, Patricia may elaborate on Patrick's precarious situation: "he has lost a lot, he has lost a situation". Necessarily. Once more, Lucienne's vindication declares that Patrick is working.

The psychic adds a layer but by using different terms: " yes, but he has been cutting his work, he is detained there, but he has plenty of determinations in his mind. "

Collocation is interesting at the beginning of life but after about fifty, it's not the same thing any more. Patrick is probably trying to release himself from this as soon as possible but only a solid financial situation allows him to do so.

According to my analysis on the psychic's thought, she is applying the following fact: that if the woman earns money, or if she controls the situation (or who rather dominates it really), a very few men would support. Which she says to Lucienne: " And to buy a big apartment, even if you give him everything, and if you wish to share everything with him euh, he is not someone who would be too willing to fight for. He is quite proud all the same. Without that, your relationship with him would have been already more lasting…. he wants to mark his territory".

These answers and Lucienne's reactions are very important at this moment since they contribute to determine the relationship with Patrick. In this case, the condition between Lucienne and Patrick seems good, without any conflicts in-between. She can thus declare, without doubt that it could be with Patrick but then she keeps an eye on this Michel whom she still doesn't know. The blow of " I see debts " also has a slight effect, with regard to Patrick's condition.

The psychic leads the discussion, she reclaims and analyzes the slightest information that her customer provides her. She uses double sided questions, any likelihood of minimizing risks and increases the chances of succeeding and ultimately, impresses her interlocutor. As soon as she acquires some information, she is careful enough not to use it at once but creates a discussion plan, in which she can deliberately spread over time. This technique allows, once applied suitably, to persuade his customer that he really had this vision. Lucienne has forgotten that she gave the information first!

If you integrate all this with the customer's expectancy situation, the fact that the psychic is only interpreting something and that people will hold on to only the right predictions, you will get hold of this psychic business. This applies to all forms of clairvoyance, palm reading, reading tea leaves or stomachs of fishes.

This example is only an example of clairvoyance by telephone, but imagine what the psychic could add to it more, once initiated to the art of body language.

- In the field of communication, the image that you reflect can be formulated, depending on how you are dressed, your jewels, hairstyle, a cold reading expert will also be equally poured into the art of discerning you "physically". The way you are dressed, the shoes that you wear, your watch, jewels, hairstyle, and everything else will be scrutinized. The quality of the ring that you are wearing can indicate your quality of life. As a matter of fact, all what you are wearing can determine you. You may thus, be competent in guessing the problems of a customer who comes in seek of a consultation by integrating all the points mentioned below:

- The person's gender, whether a man or a woman? We saw that the problems are different from each other.

- The age. Important; since considering various phases of life contribute to a good speculation along with the likelihood of proper success.

- The appearance, the image that you reflect through your dress style. Is there any difference between a person dressed in old jeans, with worn out shoes and a person dressed in a suit, with a luxury watch?

- The appearance that you throw with your body language, defines the image of an opened or a closed person, the way you sit, your look, in short, your posture that leads to acquire an idea about your disposition.

- The way you express yourself, the tone of your voice, assured or hesitating. Quite related to the previous point.

On the street, if you meet a man, well trimmed, wearing a luxury watch and a wedding ring, it will be difficult to discern what he is thinking. On the other hand if the same man appears for a clairvoyance consultation, then this will be because he seeks an answer to an important question. He is of the opinion that the only way he could come up with a solution on the circumstances of his life is to take measures in this direction. Things are at this moment different, if you recollect all the elements that we explored in this chapter. If this is a man of about forty, we can consider that he seeks for a relationship problem or maybe a divorce. It could also be regarding a change in his work. Predictions such as: *" I perceive certain type of difficulties with someone close to you, your family or at your office, someone who could generate a certain change in your life"* can lead to go hunting for information. A careful reading on limbic reactions of this man and finishing your sentence in order to imply that speaking to him can build up some contact; can influence the man to provide information. Once the information is acquired, it will then be easy to exaggerate and react in real time, similar to Patricia and Lucienne's example. If the attempt in acquiring information does not work at first, the psychic can settle on expressing some all-round phrases on the character of people. These phrases are made so as to suit to all types of people, men or women and whatever is his character. These naturally lead to obtaining information. These are sentences similar to those that

Pierre told me: *" So, Philippe I see in you a serious, determined person who always strive to attain his objectives. But there is always an interest behind all this; you are not the kind who does things without a purpose. You don't like wasting time. I also see someone who is opened to others. People do not waver to confide in you. "*

Generally, there are more non-specific sentences used, like: *" I see that you are someone kind but when you have to take matters into your own hands you can get angry ".*

These are "evasive" sentences that apply to each of us. Everybody has a part of kindness and at the same time gets angry.

The phrase that Pierre told me hits the target since he has built it up through observations that he had made during the time I had worked with him, for I had worked where he used to exercise and thus had the potential to observe me.

What is your opinion on this: "the present circumstances are favorable to you. They could adjust your attitudes towards someone close to you. It would be wrong to display any sort of indifference that could adjust your constructive relationship with the person involved."

This was today's horoscope.

Cold reading experts can make "predictions" before their customers say anything. As you can see, majority of them do not even make the simplest effort and directly ask their customers for details of their visits!

Do you remember the flash that my friend Pierre had about my girlfriend during the time? How did he do it? How did Anne perceive the number on my license plate? Do you know how?

Before examining on that, **I am about to show you in a few pages a method where the person who speaks to you forgets his own words**. Don't go dreaming, for we are not in the "Men in Black" movie.

But before doing so, here is a small exercise. I will transcribe to you, the second session with Patricia, which you will be analyzing. Note down the important information from the beginning and try to draw up a discussion plan. Note down the statements with probability, those that were successful. Next, we shall together examine this famous technique that is in fact certainly used in this session.

→ *The psychic, still being Patricia, welcomes the second person: "hello.*

→ *Hello Patricia, I am calling from Essonne (a French area) and I am 51 years old, I'd like to know, I applied for several housing applications so as to change my region. And my question is to verify if these applications would soon succeed?*

→ *Alright, could you give me your first name?*

→ *Sandrine.*

→ *(Psychic's thought) and so you are in Essonne... Oh, who is there within twenty kilometers of Essonne?*

→ *Within twenty kilometers? Hm... Ah! My ex-husband is there.*

→ *All right ... euh tell me, about your files, were they made by the city hall?*

→ *No, I applied them since I was looking for a job in the south-east at the same time and I applied for my housing all together. Well, I am still unemployed but above all, I would also like to know if I am going to have the housing, as a matter of fact, one conditions the other.*

→ *But why do I see the city hall all the time? And, the housing, isn't it related to the city hall?*

→ *Generally no, there are social welfare bodies but I didn't apply them to the city hall*

→ *All right ... (thinks), hm ... It's going to be a little long, Sandrine. This is strange because I see two places; one may perhaps not please you but could be made faster. It is as though it could have two proposals there.*

→ *All right.*

→ *There is one maybe towards the end of the year and the other is perhaps on February or March but the other is in the city and is not so big, I have the impression that concerning work this is will please you.*

→ *Ah, all right.*

→ *Since this will have a relationship with your work and the rest and everything.*

→ *Ah I have not yet found a job, but possibly, will it be in the city hall? Perhaps that's what you are speaking about ?*

→ *Yes, since I see a big structure, I perceive there is a bit of a white in the structure, euh, white coat or something similar and however, it is related to the others, humanely, and the city is not a big city either. It is a little like countryside, but it smells like pine!*

→ *Ah!*

→ *So, have you heard about it?*

→ *Euh, yes, I had had an interview in the south-east, but it didn't turn out well, will they call me back then, because it's in the medical sector. And, since you are telling me about some white coat, here we are, but there is already someone recruited and so, I don't think if it's that.*

→ *Ah, Sandrine, I am obliged to repeat, do not leave...hm, who is Marie?*

→ *Marie, euh I have no idea who that is.*

→ *Isn't it this woman there?*

→ *No, her name is not Marie, no.*

→ *Keep Marie aside for a while, I am not sure if this person will keep her post, since I am not sure if she corresponds with places where there are white coats.*

→ *Ah all right, I might have a chance then. Since, they had wavered a lot between the two of us for this post.*

→ *That's it, I advised to you eh, this is really an advice since I really feel it.... it would be good that you keep in touch, to imply that you are also expecting.*

→ *All right, well, I'll listen to your advice.*

→ *Yes, yes I feel it, really.*

→ *Great, and therefore, for my housing, perhaps I should pass by the city hall then?*

→ *Ah but I see the city hall all the time. The city hall or someone in the city hall will help you to find a housing.*

→ *Well, I hope it comes fast because I've already given my advance notice and that's also why I called you to make sure if I should cancel my advance notice or not.*

→ *I tell you, there, where you met, this person you see, I can't say if she is going to stay. This is a*

person who is not nice but there will be more
empathy towards you, so don't give up, Sandrine
➔ *All right, thanks a lot. "*

The session concludes.

What couldn't you detect through the excellent cold reading? You must have certainly noticed the sudden flashes "who is there within twenty kilometers?" and the rest of the possibilities that it can cover. The emphasis on the city hall, a bit similar to the Michel in the previous session. You must have also observed « I see two places, one may perhaps not please you.... »

It is as though it could have two proposals..... The city that is not so big, must be certainly reminding you about the blow where the floor is not too high in the previous example. A relationship with your work, always has big chances of hitting the target.

This session becomes more interesting with the evocation of a structure with a bit of a white inside. Right away, we are inclined to think of a hospital but in fact, it can suit many things. The building could be candy pink but the white entrance hall is used.

Patricia tries a bluff by speaking about white coats. Besides, there are quite a lot of possibilities, my butcher wears a white coat, and moreover, you must have noticed that the psychic mentions nothing about a hospital. Afterwards, Patricia does not continue to bother herself by seeking more information but directly asks her customer if her interpretation reminds her of something. And it turned out just right! Her customer had applied for a medical profession where obviously, there are men and women in white coats.

Et voila.

Here is a very satisfactory example of "a one-in-ten success" which is going to strengthen the reputation of this psychic even more. Should the opposite occur; Patricia would have answered in this way: "hum, however, this is strange for I see white coats, carefully recollect on it, might have something to do with what you are looking for, possibly not directly but it will have a relationship ".

For example.

If cold reading is a set of techniques contributing to implicitly acquire information of a person, clairvoyance professions require reading potentials and constant analysis. They must be aware that it is through another's body language as in the analysis of his words that information can be disclosed. Information which must then be applied and manipulated so as to divulge another information. And so on, up to the signature on the check... Since all that we have just seen can be based on areas other than psychics or communicating with the dead. Because this is about mental manipulations. You decided to buy yourself a car, new or second-hand and you go to the city dealer. Let us assume that the seller is a cold manipulator. He will not be predicting your future obviously, but somehow try to sell you a vehicle. Through the visual analysis that you cast, for example the car that you were driving at the moment, will give him a good idea of what you are looking for. As you see it, do you think he will offer you the same vehicle if you turn up with the wheel of an old car or if your neighbor lent you his Porsche? The fact that whether you are a man or a woman as well as your age are also indications for the seller. Did you come with your children, your son? How do you know that the magnificent vehicle that is accidentally found right in front of you in the garage courtyard was not put there according to his cold reading ability (and introduced as if to boast about all its advantages) taking care to ignore or devalue other cheaper vehicles?
A seller can very well ask you questions to acquire more information from you (this is not about clairvoyance) and observe your limbic reactions, determine if you seem conquered or if you should be directed into another vehicle. You are in a state of expectancy, and the car seller who tells you that the engine is in perfect condition disguises himself similar to the psychic who

alone can interpret cards. Unless you are a mechanic you know nothing about the engine. Nevertheless, your brain is permanently attacked by the image right in front of you conveying that this vehicle is in perfect condition. Thus, will I get a great deal? Is it really in good condition? However, it looks quite very attractive. Have you never had inner conflicts between what you think and the appearances that are right in front of you?

This clairvoyance example is an excellent precedent for mental manipulation. Consequently, you will naturally be proficient in detecting when someone tries to coat you with his sales pitch. Take time to think in depth about the visual impact concept that I shared with you in my cold reading chapter. Since our childhood, we have been in touch with the TV that has a violent impact on our brain. Undoubtedly. But as we grew up with time, we begin to be less concerned on the visual impact of the images on our brain. And even more on the impact of what we daily see. Our brain sees everything all at once and records them all.

Well and after all this, how had Anne seen the number on my license plate? How did Pierre get it right about my girlfriend? How can it lead to make someone forget his own words?

Coming up in the next chapter...

Chapter 5

<u>MENTAL MANIPULATIONS</u>

In this chapter we will be exploring on various mental manipulations. You have clearly understood that I do not discuss about paranormal, and we are not psychically going to influence the thoughts of the other people but instead, use these techniques that will successfully contribute to achieve that task. In mentalism, you may have already heard about misdirections, which are techniques that deviate attention. In my cold reading technique, I approached the concept of thought diversion. Hence, here, we will first elaborate on this. Moreover, we shall approach on planning or how to persuade someone that the events occurring to him are due to chance. Next, we will examine the technique that leads your interlocutor to forget his own words.

In order to investigate into all this I suggest you begin to study a classic case which we have already come across if you have ventured on lie detection.

Let us imagine that you saw on TV; someone known, a political personality or some popular entertainment figure who expresses his opinion about a charge that would be carried against him.

"No, I didn't do any of these things for which I am accused of "

he says to the journalists. And at this very moment you saw a limbic reaction, a sudden look, and you found in his words something faulty. Shortly, this is a signal which reminds you that this person is lying. Despite this; he claims the opposite. The following morning, when you go to your work, you see this matter disclosed in newsstands: "Mr. X denies the facts for which he is accused". Then, on the Internet also, you see this information. And then again in the evening news as well. But this time, it's this personality's lawyer who expresses himself: "no, my customer has never done anything worth being accused ". You found a signal in this person, but even then, he declares the opposite, his lawyer declares the opposite and the rest of the media as well. Furthermore, it seems so surprising on behalf of this personality; after all I was there when it happened? Do I have any proof? Well I must have made a mistake then. As one would tend to think. If images have a certain impact on the brain, then so does sound. Your brain equally captures sounds and words that it hears without you realizing it. Even when you are not consciously listening. Of course, this takes a little more than images since it must chain the words that are interpreted during the time period. An image on the other hand is wrapped up within seconds by your right brain that, I repeat, processes the data in a holistic approach, which is to say, all at once. Thus, unconsciously, you acquire all this information, those broadcasted by the media, Lawyer's words etc. Then, you will see and capture this information for several days and this massive amount of information will eventually arouse doubts in you.

Consequently, who is right? You or your appearances? We come across many such examples very frequently.

For example, a study demonstrates that the use of mobile phones can damage your health. This information is broadcasted through media; you read it, analyze it and admit the fact that it can be true. After all it was scientists, engineers or experts who brought this out. Then, shortly after, what is discovered? Studies also carried out by experts, who demonstrated the opposite! The first information finds itself in no time, drowned in the middle of the contradictory information creating a sort of general doubt bearing on the question.

Hence, in the example of the personality who proclaims his innocence, it won't be surprising if you doubt. However, I invite you to persevere and look for other indications that can be added to the first one. On one hand it will encourage you, and on the other, it will maintain your critical and analytical mind at a certain level. This is not about declaring whether you are right just because you detected a lie, but you have to manipulate your examinations against these appearances and look for other indications.

If it is about events that taking place in your life, where there is a risk of having a big change, I encourage you to never give up your investigations, unless of course, the obvious proof that could contradict your analysis has been acquired.

We discerned a good example on social conflict that took place in the company that I work for. This old gentleman with a pleasant appearance whose images transmitted by him were contradictory to the general atmosphere. An effective example on mental manipulation, that involves changing the impression that someone conveys to you by playing on the visual impact. These types of mental manipulations are found everywhere. Even in boxing for example. Certain boxers wear a mouth guard on which there have black teeth drawn. When he opens his mouth; it looks like nearly one half of the teeth are missing and the visual impact is immediate on his opponent's brain. Quite similar when the gong at the of the end of rest period (between rounds) rings, and a certain boxer gets up immediately conveying the visual impact of someone ready to fight (not even tired) in the brain of their still seated opponents. Yes, body language tricks are also present in sports. And who said body language tricks means creating an image that is conveyed to your interlocutor within seconds.

In order to expand a certain insight on this manipulation technique, practice the following tricks regularly.

When you are traveling or seated quietly in a park, observe people around you. Then observe one person in particular. Do not analyze this person at once; anyway, it is now too late as your brain has already captured this image. Now stop looking at this person. Look for the impression or feelings that this person inspired you. Now use your left brain, the logical, analytical and sequential mind to analyze this person. Scrutinize her slightest details, all her clothes that she is wearing, her jewels, her hairstyle, her physical appearance, in brief everything. Do you find any correspondence or a difference with your first impressions?

Next observe her posture, her body movements, and her body language. Does she render an impression of an open or closed person? Does she look tightened or relaxed, in brief try to have an idea of her disposition. Compare these data once more with your first impressions.

Now, add to it the background.
Is this a man or a woman? What might be her age? What's the time? Is it 8.00 am in the morning and are you traveling to work? Is it late afternoon and is this person sitting quietly on a chair in the park?

Now, try to guess what she is doing there. Why is she there?
Now with all this information, try to guess her thoughts. What are the thoughts of this woman seated on the patio of a coffee bar looking out at the people in the street?
Do a constant observation and indications will come into view.

If you practice this exercise regularly, you will attain the proficiency to analyze very successfully And hence, control a critical situation within a second.

Planning

In my previous book, I introduced the art of ground preparation. How to create an atmosphere and set up particular psychological elements in order to build a trap and thus, effectively frame the person who should confess the truth to you or otherwise make him confess.

Unless that we lie to ourselves it is to others that we lie and the key element that must be adjusted in order to make a lie invisible, is the routine.
It can seem simple but certain people are perceptible to changes that may intervene into their lives. A few paranoiac or jealous people will find it very doubtful if their spouse suddenly begins to

go out in the evening while until then, she/he found pleasure in staying at home.

It is the technique that can contribute, not to directly detect a lie but to indicate you that there has been a change in habits. I call it the "change in the flow".

Days, weekends, weeks, months always the same thing happens. Your wife leaves in the morning for work at 8:30 am and returns at about 7 pm. This is the daily routine and suddenly she returns at 8.00 pm several times a week. On the first evening you asked her about her delay and she answered that she had more work. It is possible but if this had never come across before, then it becomes an element worth taking into consideration as a change of pattern and to correlate with other indications that you would eventually collect. Let us take an example on planning. For a little change, I will not refer to cheating among couples but an example of a husband who wishes to give a beautiful surprise to his lover by organizing her a birthday surprise. Problem; last year he entirely and simply forgot the date. As the fateful day approaches, this woman will become even more suspicious and observe the slightest actions of her husband.

She knows his routine well, she is aware that he drives his car to work at 8.00 am and he always returns at about 5.30-5.45 depending on the traffic. The weekend is normally spent together. Imagine that it's Monday and the birthday is on Friday. The husband thought of a good present for her but he must set up a suitable time to go to the store and buy it. He also wants to find a good restaurant where he will invite some of her friends without her knowing it. A little time will not be enough to visit various restaurants. Imagine that this man returns home at about 7 pm during three days during this week. With his wife watching him, the speculations will be obvious. So, how can it be done? Thus, the key element; 'the routine' must be adjusted. An element must be incorporated into the flow of his daily life which will become a routine over time and hence will eventually go unnoticed by his wife.

In order to accomplish this, a new element must be implemented much more early. One month earlier, the husband can declare that he will be starting on a new project and will have to stay a little late in the evening for at least once a week. We are not going to study all the possibilities, this is only a simple example, but I am certain you have understood the principle. If the wife believes the fact that he will be late once a week, then that's exactly what is needed, the element is now combined and has become a part of the routine. The husband will now have the freedom of doing as he wished. With the intention of rendering an example on planning, the husband could thus, consult several web sites for vehicle servicing, approximately one week before. He would arrange this, in case his wife pulls out trouble. The husband **must** ignore his wife, it is not **he** who should show her these sites but **she** who should take the initiative and ask why he is consulting them. This is quite important since the wife must be led to think that it is herself who took the initiative. The husband can then answer her doubts that his car battery level was low and that he had difficulty in starting his car, before leaving for work. The day of the birthday, while leaving for work, the husband can then go back to the apartment and disgustedly ask his wife if she can transport him to the office and come looking for him in the evening. The husband can disconnect the battery and show to his wife that the car really does not start.

This is a way of attracting her towards the restaurant for example.

But that is not the point, have you comprehended the concept? You instilled your wife with an element that has nothing to do with her birthday. Just another day, that's it. Nothing more and you won't speak about it any more. And it will seem normal to her.

Another example; you mentioned to one of your friends that you were a mentalist, and that you could see certain things. You suggest speaking about it with him in a small restaurant this evening.

You tell your friend: "I will let you choose the restaurant."

You go to it, and in the middle of the meal you bet with your friend that you can cold read the waitress and guess her first name. And this is exactly what you do !

There would be just enough time for you to walk up to the restaurant an hour before, enter into it and ask for information and note down everything that would appear susceptible to be a clairvoyance gift, something that we see only from the counter, for example or maybe the first name of a waitress. This can very well show up when her boss calls her for example or when you are nearby. Afterwards, you leave. You will even have the audacity to show up late by calling your friend and informing that you are stuck in the traffic or that you have difficulty in finding the street of the restaurant since you have no GPS. You create a convincing story for your friend by using elements such as; traffic jams or GPS. Which he will indeed accept without any doubt. The effect is thus, guaranteed.

Do you remember Pierre's prediction about my girlfriend at the time? As she visited regularly with a friend of hers to the fitness gym that I used to work, Pierre had just heard a conversation about her financial problems. Isn't that an exquisite flash?

And what about Anne and her vision on my license plate number? I confess to you, It took me a certain amount of time before understand the situation.

What I noticed was that she came out to have a cigarette during her breaks after each consultation. And she was certainly in the street as I drove in with my car. She knew my age, and very few cars were passing by in her street which was quite small. There was enough time for her to stand out there and note my number, before the appointment time. But what if I had not have parked in this street? Nothing serious, then she would not make the flash but isn't it worth trying?

Does she do this to all her customers? Without doubt, but I cannot confirm it. Excellent, don't you think? In order to gain a high reputation, this is very well thought of. Once the trick is disclosed, it seems quite simple but when you are totally unaware, that's when it does its magic! Imagine those customers who are in states of expectancies that we discussed earlier, who believe that the psychic that they are about to consult is renowned for his flashes. That whatever he predicts will be the interpretation of signs from elsewhere and that these customers are going to hold on to only what answers their questions…

An outstanding aspect for this manipulation, however.

And have we examined on the technique that leads to make someone forget his own words?

Obviously, it doesn't always work but I have done it accidentally when I added some pressure on someone who wouldn't stop changing the subject when we were discussing something important. And I believe that Patricia, the psychic is also applying it. I am not sure though, if it's consciously done. Let us return to the person who had come with her problems to consult Patricia. Recollect yourself on the whole manipulation process that we have just discussed. And return to the psychic's second session with a customer called Sandrine. After a while the psychic sees the place where Sandrine could be brought to work, a little like countryside but smells of pine! Sandrine seems surprised by what she has just heard because she had precisely applied for a job in the south-east where there is a strong likelihood of having pines. What a vision! But it's quite obvious that Sandrine, had revealed this information much earlier in the discussion, which she fails to remember any longer. Once you get ready to render explanations to someone, as in Sandrine's case who gets ready to speak to the psychic, you quickly organize the points that you will be saying by trying to memorize them.

Precisely, like for the last minutes just before a job interview. Thus, for the manipulation to work, thoughts must be more or less directly discontinued. Doing so, will break the flow of his words along with his thoughts at the moment. Then, it is promptly necessary to deviate your interlocutor's attention to somewhere else but especially to make him think of something quite different.

This is why Patricia repeatedly continues to speak about the city hall. Sandrine then gives her the information saying that she is looking for a job in the southeast but the psychic at once continues with the city hall: "but why I see this city hall all the time? ". Sandrine is instantly deviated from her reflection. Then the psychic starts again by creating a scenario with both possibilities, on when it could be done, etc…

Thus, she succeeds in taking over Sandrine's mind.
A blow like: "Who is Michel? " interrupts the person who was talking about something else and thus breaks her reflection process and in addition, she is forced to focus on something quite different like looking for Michel in her life. The way of saying "Who is Michel " is also important, you need to render the impression that you were not listening to what your interlocutor has just told you. This was very well done by Patricia. Not in an unfriendly manner of course, but as if she was absorbed in her clairvoyance and busy with her visions. This will reflect in the customer's mind, unconsciously **of course**, the feeling that she had not even uttered her words. Since the psychic had not heard them. Interrupting the flow of reflection, changing the subject immediately to something else, taking over his mind and further for a short while, leads your interlocutor **to forget the information that he had revealed**.

Do not forget the scope, the process and all the manipulations that are enclosed within a session. Hence, you will attain a greater likelihood of success.

Here, we have reached the end of this chapter. These are only some examples but these techniques can be extended easily.

This is a vast and complex subject and I hope that this chapter will offer you an insight to thoughts and observations.

CONCLUSIONS

I hope that this book succeeded in enlightening you.

It is focused on increasing your potential in analyzing another, which stands to be a dominant feature in lie detection. My cold reading technique had not only served me on the case of social conflict but has also helped me whenever I needed to disentangle the truth from forgery, both in my personal life as during the inquiries on which I have investigated.

Thus, you have learned some manipulation techniques used in mentalism, art of manipulating the other, and also the art of feigning psychic powers.

Perhaps, you might become a psychic yourself?

If this new modest small book has rendered you with something, and if it has contributed to increase your circumspection to a better level; hence, you shall see me quite delighted.

Here's a list below, of my two other books about lie detection:

www.ingramcontent.com/pod-product-compliance
Lightning Source LLC
Chambersburg PA
CBHW062016280526
45787CB00005B/2120